ISBN 978-1-334-20350-3
PIBN 10755966

1 MONTH OF
FREE
READING

at
www.ForgottenBooks.com

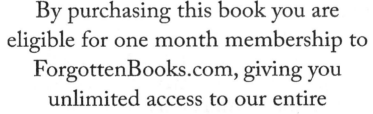

By purchasing this book you are eligible for one month membership to ForgottenBooks.com, giving you unlimited access to our entire collection of over 1,000,000 titles via our web site and mobile apps.

To claim your free month visit:
www.forgottenbooks.com/free755966

English
Français
Deutsche
Italiano
Español
Português

www.forgottenbooks.com

Mythology Photography **Fiction**
Fishing Christianity **Art** Cooking
Essays Buddhism Freemasonry
Medicine **Biology** Music **Ancient
Egypt** Evolution Carpentry Physics
Dance Geology **Mathematics** Fitness
Shakespeare **Folklore** Yoga Marketing
Confidence Immortality Biographies
Poetry **Psychology** Witchcraft
Electronics Chemistry History **Law**
Accounting **Philosophy** Anthropology
Alchemy Drama Quantum Mechanics
Atheism Sexual Health **Ancient History**
Entrepreneurship Languages Sport
Paleontology Needlework Islam
Metaphysics Investment Archaeology
Parenting Statistics Criminology
Motivational

A

FAREWELL SERMON.

PREACHED AT

BRAINTREE, MASS. ⌐

ON

'LORD'S DAY, MAY 7, 1809.

BEING

THE SABBATH AFTER HIS PASTORAL AND MINISTE-
RIAL RELATION TO THE CHURCH AND CON-
GREGATION WAS DISSOLVED, BY AN
ECCLESIASTICAL COUNCIL
MUTUALLY CHOSEN.

———⋑ഠഠഠഠഠ⋐———

BY SYLVESTER SAGE.
———⋑ഠഠഠഠ⋐———

PUBLISHED AT THE PARTICULAR REQUEST OF THE SUBSCRIBERS.

Boston :
PRINTED BY MANNING & LORING, No. 2, CORNHILL.
1809.

Presented   Col. Ha den of Brain

FAREWELL SERMON.

———————

WE are assembled, perhaps, for the last time, until we meet at the bar of our Omniscient Judge. As this is the last opportunity I expect to have to address you upon the interesting subject of salvation, so it may be the last you will have to hear me : therefore, let our united prayers ascend to the throne of infinite purity, that I may be enabled to speak, as a dying man to dying men : and that you may, with candour, hear the parting counsel of one who earnestly desireth your souls' prosperity.

The words I have selected for the foundation of the present discourse, you will find in

THE ACTS OF THE APOSTLES, xviii. 11.

AND HE CONTINUED THERE A YEAR AND SIX MONTHS, TEACHING THE WORD OF GOD AMONG THEM.

These words were spoken concerning Paul; and they express the length of time he continued at Corinth, and the business in which he was employed, teaching the word of God : and it is believed they may lead our attention to some things not unsuitable, but highly proper, on this solemn occasion.

Two general ideas are obviously contained in the words of the text, to which we shall, by divine leave, endeavour to attend.

I. The great business of a minister among the people with whom he is connected. And

II. That however short the time of any minister's labours among a people, yet that time is important.

The business of a minister is to teach the word of God. In which duty we may note two things.

1. The business: *Teaching.* In this is implied exposition of the scriptures. The scriptures of the Old and New Testament are what he is to explain to his people in his public discourses. The word of God is the treasury of truth; from which the minister is, from time to time, to draw out things to alarm the careless; to direct the inquiring; to comfort the afflicted, and to quicken and animate the children of God in the discharge of duty. He must be cautious not to put any false interpretation upon any part of scripture, but to let scripture be its own expositor; or, in other words, to put no construction upon any passage that is contrary, but rather that which is according to the general current of the sacred volume. In the exposition of scripture, the faithful minister will find it necessary to point the arrows of the law against all the wicked, and denounce the thunders of Sinai against every impenitent sinner. He can never cry peace and safety to the wicked, when sudden destruction cometh. Nay, he will explain and enforce, with all the cogency of language, those important truths contained in the Bible; all which are of consequence to be known, rightly understood, and cordially embraced by every individual of his charge. In his expositions of scripture, he will endeavour, not only to alarm the secure, but to instruct the inquiring; will lead them to a view of Christ, and giving them no encouragement of safety while out of Christ Jesus, the gospel ark. He will never prophesy smooth things to lull his people into security: for his commission declares, "There is no peace to the wicked;" but he will explain the scriptures, as giving not the least encouragement to sin, nor any ground to hope for happiness beyond the grave, only in the sovereign grace of God, though the merits of Jesus Christ.

The minister of Jesus is not only to teach by expounding the sacred scriptures, in his public discourses, but by his example. "Be thou an example of the believers," said Paul to Timothy. It is no less a true than a common saying, example teaches more powerfully than precept. It is evident from experience and observation, that however faithfully and clearly the scriptures are explained by a minister, if his example be not good, he will not only destroy all the good his expositions and instructions would have been calculated to produce, had his example been such as becometh the gospel; but will have influence on the minds of sinners, and serve to lead them into open infidelity. When his people see him regardless of his own instructions, and manifesting an open inattention to the solemn injunctions of the divine word, they will readily say, Our minister certainly does not believe it to be important, nor even necessary, to live according to the directions of the Bible; if he did, he would not exhibit such an example before us of disobedience to the divine word. He does not conduct in conformity to the rules of scripture, as he explains them to us; therefore he does not believe them himself; and as it is agreeable to our natural inclinations, we also will disregard them. Although he has taught us repeatedly, that we must be benevolent, and forgive those who have injured us, or we cannot be the children of our Father who is in heaven; and indeed we cannot deny this to be a duty plainly and repeatedly inculcated in the word of God; yet he does not set us an example of obedience, and as it will gratify our dispositions, we will follow his example, instead of his precepts.

It is as important that a minister exhibit a good example, as that he truly expound the scriptures. For if his example contradict his preaching, the probability is, both will be worse than in vain, and serve to harden his people in wickedness. It is an undeniable truth, that every minister of Jesus Christ, who hath any just sense of the importance of the scriptures he expounds, will also feel the indispensable obligations upon him to exhibit a Christian example. In this way he will cause his light to shine, that others beholding his good works, his pious and holy example, may be induced to glorify God.

He will also teach by his conversation. In private conversation, the minister can be more familiar, and come more near to the peculiar cases of his people; can better adapt his discourse to their circumstances, than is practicable in his public addresses. His conversation among his people ought always to be savory, pure and serious. It never should be vain and idle, calculated to render useless his public instructions; but, on the contrary, such as will be in accordance with truth, and serve to recommend the pure doctrines of the gospel to the attention and acceptance of those with whom he converses. The direction of Paul to Timothy was, " Be thou an example of the believers in word, in *conversation*, in charity, in spirit, in faith, in purity." Hence the duty of a holy conversation in all the ministers of Jesus Christ. The same apostle, writing to Titus, said, " In all things showing thyself a pattern of good works ; in doctrine showing uncorruptness, gravity, sincerity, sound speech that cannot be condemned ; that he that is of the contrary part may be ashamed, having no evil thing to say of you." Thus a minister is to teach his people in a threefold manner : by a solemn exposition of the sacred scriptures, by a holy example, and by a pious conversation.

We may note

2. The subject matter of his instructions ; *The word of God.*

The word of God contains all those doctrines, commands, precepts, prohibitions, promises and threatenings which are to be found in the Bible. These are all to be taught by a minister to his people, as time and opportunity shall admit. All these things must be brought to clear view, even should not his continuance with his people give him opportunity to dwell particularly upon every distinct subject. The sacred scripture, which is the word of God, is an extensive field from which the minister may gather and bring to his people, things suitable for them in every condition. In that field, every thing may be found that is necessary. There is meat for men ; milk for babes ; medicine for the sick ; strength for the weak ; instruction for the ignorant ; succour for the tempted ; and an infallible direction for every weary traveller who is passing through the wilderness of this world to Mount Zion. There are way marks erected, and directions given, impossible to be misunderstood by any one who is really desirous to know and understand the right way. And, as expressed by the prophet Isaiah, " The wayfaring men, though fools, shall not err therein."

In teaching the word of God, a minister will bring the divine character into clear view, and exhibit God as a being possessed of every adorable attribute and glorious perfection ; being one in essence, and yet subsisting in three undivided persons ; according to the declaration of an inspired apostle, 1 John v. 7. " For there are three that bear record in heaven, the Father, the Word, and the Holy Ghost : and these three are one." However high and mysterious the doctrine of the Trinity in Unity may be to us, creatures but of yesterday, as it is a doctrine revealed, it must be declared ; and indeed it will be, by every faithful minister of God our Saviour. The godhead of the Father, of the Son, and of the Holy Ghost must be true, or the scheme of salvation, revealed in the gospel, must be deficient, and can never answer the purposes for which it was intended.

The character of the Father, Son, and Holy Ghost, the one God, is pure and holy. This God possesseth the glorious attributes of wisdom, power, holiness, justice, goodness and truth. He is omniscient and omnipresent, and exerciseth an universal government over all worlds ; requiring cordial obedience of all his rational creatures in all parts of his extensive dominions. As God is infinite in being and perfection, is the creator and preserver of all things, so he is the Governor and Disposer of all creatures, actions and things, by his most wise and holy providence ; working all things after the coun-sel of his own will.

Another truth in the word of God, the minister will teach his people, is, that although man was made after the image of him who created him, in knowledge, righteousness, and true holiness, yet hath, by transgression, fallen from his primitive state, become wholly destitute of God's moral image, and deserving of endless wrath. It is evi-dent that all men, naturally, possess that "carnal mind which is enmity against God, which is not subject to the law of God, neither indeed can be." This truth, however wounding to human pride, and however much it may expose the minister to the jeer and contempt of those who have never seen the awful depravity of their own hearts, he will, in a plain and solemn manner, exhibit to the view of his people ; for he must know, that unless they become sensible that "they are wretched, and miserable, and poor, and blind, and naked," and flee to the gospel ark, they must perish in the deluge of divine wrath. Love to God, and to the souls of his people, will in-duce him to use plainness of speech on this subject.

The minister will also feel it his duty to teach this scripture truth, that although men are rebels against the King of heaven, they are capable of knowing and doing the whole of their duty, were their hearts but suitably disposed : consequently are proper sub-jects of God's moral government, and without ex-cuse for every degree of sin. There is no inability under which men labour, that will in any degree excuse them ; because the whole difficulty lieth in disaffection of heart to God ; in an indisposition to comply with gospel requirements, and in a heart fully set in them to do evil.

Another prominent doctrine of the Bible is, that God could not, consistently with his law and charac-ter, save an individual of the apostate race of men without an atonement. "Without shedding of blood is no remission." Christ, the second person in the adorable trinity, did undertake the business; offered himself as a sacrifice for sin, by which offering he hath made it consistent for the Father to justify every one who believeth in his Son Jesus Christ, and opened up a new way of life, out of which there is no salvation for an individual of Adam's guilty race. This plainly revealed doctrine, the minister will teach his people in the most affectionate manner, knowing it to be a truth essentially necessary for them to understand and believe.

He will also teach them another, no less important doctrine of the word of God. That although the way is opened, and all are invited, yea, even commanded, to return to God through Christ, that they may live; yet all men are naturally so opposed to God, in their hearts, and to the scheme of salvation by Jesus Christ, which exalts God and humbles the creature, that they will forever perish, unless prevented by the sovereign grace of that God who "hath mercy on whom he will have mercy."

In connexion with this, he will also teach, that God, in holy sovereignty, in his own time and way, by the energetic operation of his Holy Spirit, will draw to Jesus Christ all those to whom he will give eternal life; and that this is wholly of God's free, rich, and abounding grace. "Not of works, lest any man should boast." That regeneration, or being born again, is a change wrought in the heart of man, by the agency of the Holy Ghost; and that such is the native enmity of the carnal mind against God, not an individual of mankind can ever be admitted into the kingdom of heaven, unless he is made to experience this change, and to possess, in this life, a holy temper of heart.

The minister of Christ will not only state and prove the afore-mentioned doctrines of God's word, but will also endeavour to enforce them upon his people by the solemn considerations of a general resurrection of the dead, and a future judgment; at which time all true believers in Jesus will be received into the everlasting joys of their Lord, and all who live and die impenitent in sin shall be rejected, and consigned over to endless punishment; " Who shall be punished with everlasting destruction from the presence of the Lord, and from the glory of his power."

The truths that have been brought to view are not doubtful, although they are much disputed; for they are written, as with a sun-beam, in the volume of sacred inspiration; and one would think they must be seen by every candid searcher after moral truth; and they will be cordially loved and embraced by every pious mind.

The minister of Jesus, from a sense of duty to his God, to his people, and to his own soul, will not shun to declare all the revealed counsel of Heaven. This he will endeavour to do, " not in the words which man's wisdom teacheth, but which the Holy Ghost teacheth ; comparing spiritual things with spiritual." Feeling desirous of being a humble instrument, in the hand of God, of promoting the divine glory, in the salvation of his dear people, he will study to preach the unadulterated *word of God ;* in opposition to tradition. Although he may avail himself of the best expositors, yet he will be careful to call no man father; and he will follow none where he imagines they depart from the simplicity of the gospel. All traditionary notions and pre-conceived opinions which will not bear examination by the light of truth, will find no place in his discourses ; but he will reject them as mere rubbish, compared with the truths so prominent in the gospel revelation.

The true minister of Jesus will also preach the word of God in opposition to heresy and impure mixtures. He will be careful not to corrupt the word, by endeavouring to make it speak a language contrary to its most plain and obvious meaning. It will be his prayerful solicitude to light his lamp at the pure source of truth; that the light of doctrine he communicates may be pure and bright; that it may shine with steady though increasing lustre, and not be eclipsed with any heresy, or rendered variable by any impure ingredients.

Carnal reasoning he will reject, as not tending to godly edifying. Remembering that "cursed be he that doth the work of the Lord deceitfully," it will be his studious and prayerful endeavour to be found faithful. Like holy Paul, he will be bold in his God to speak to his people the gospel of God with much engagedness, that he may be able to adopt the apostolic language, and say, " My exhortation was not of deceit, nor of uncleanness, nor in guile : but as I was allowed of God to be put in trust with the gospel, even so I speak, not as pleasing men, but God, who trieth my heart."

It will be his study to teach his people the whole system of Christian doctrines and duties, in opposition to partiality. He will not dare to dwell solely on some more plain and easy subjects, while he neglects others more difficult. Those doctrines that serve to exalt free and sovereign grace, and tend to humble the pride of man ; which serve to show man his true character as a rebel against God, and the only way of salvation through a crucified Saviour, however contrary to the wishes of his people, and the feelings of the corrupt heart, he will not shun to teach and declare, with great plainness of speech ; because he feels himself accountable to his Lord and Master, for the manner in which he discharges his ministerial functions. Thus he will, if faithful, teach the word of God to every man, and warn every man ; and will be careful to do nothing by partiality, that he may approve himself to God, and to every man's conscience as in the sight of God.

We pass to consider, as proposed,

II. That however short the time of any minister's labours among a people, yet that time is important.

The truth of this proposition is evident from this single consideration, viz. If it were not important, the particular time of Paul's continuance at Corinth

would not have been mentioned in the sacred scriptures, where nothing is mentioned in vain. But
here it becomes us to consider in what respects the
time of a minister's continuance among a people is
important. It is so in various respects :

1st. Because by teaching in the manner above
mentioned, something of God's glorious character,
and plan of grace by Jesus Christ are manifested.
In teaching the word, it is impossible but that the
character of God should be brought to view; for it
is God's word that is taught. Whenever we are
conversant with any writings, we generally learn
something of the character of their author, by the
subjects they contain, and the manner in which he
treats them; even though nothing particularly re-
lating to his character should be expressed. But es-
pecially should we learn it, if the writer had been
particular in his description of himself. That God
hath done this, in his word, every page in that sacred
book testifieth; and that teacher of the word, who is
engaged rightly to divide the word of truth, cannot
fail in every discourse, either explicitly or implicitly
to bring into view some one or more perfection be-
longing to God's glorious character. In the plan of
grace, by Jesus Christ, the character of God shines
with peculiar brightness, as a God of boundless compassion and mercy, as well as of justice and truth.
In this wonderful scheme into which angels desire
to look, the wisdom, power, and goodness of God
are displayed; and the teacher of the word cannot
but dwell with enraptured delight upon that glorious
plan of grace, by Jesus Christ, revealed in the gospel,
for the salvation of apostate men, which might well
astonish angelic hosts.

That preacher who can, from sabbath to sabbath
pass along, without bringing to view the purity and
holiness of God; his opposition to all sin, and his
determination to punish it; his love of holiness,
and designs of mercy to the penitent; who can
neglect saying any thing respecting the divinity of
Christ, which would give his people to understand

what his sentiments of Christ are, must meet with much difficulty; for these truths will meet him on every page of that word he pretends to teach; and it must require much ingenuity, and no less disaffection of heart to the true scheme of grace by Jesus Christ, to teach things which serve to bring the demands of the law and gospel down to the feelings of corrupt nature, and the character of God our Saviour on a level with that of man. Such will not be the teaching of a true minister of Jesus Christ; but, however short the time may be of his continuance among a people, God's true character, and the gospel scheme of grace, will be brought to view in a clear, scriptural light, and held up to them in the most affectionate and engaging manner.

2d. Because the terms of acceptance with God are proposed for their reception.

To those who live where the light of the gospel never shined, and where no information respecting the character of God, the plan of salvation, and the terms of acceptance with the Lord is communicated, except what is learned from the light of nature, time, comparatively, is of little importance. But to those who live under gospel light; who do or might enjoy continual opportunities of learning the way of life; who have the terms of acceptance with God presented before them, and are urged by all the most powerful arguments and motives to comply, every moment is precious, and ought to be rightly improved. Every individual, who lives where the gospel is faithfully preached, hath the terms of acceptance with God proposed to him, even though he should be so abandoned to sin, that he will not come to the house of worship to hear. He must be accountable, not only for what he did hear, but also for all he might have heard, of the way of life and salvation by Jesus Christ.

In the preaching of the gospel, repentance and faith are proclaimed as the terms of salvation, or as those exercises without which salvation can never be obtained.

Sinners are urged to these exercises, by every motive that can influence an ingenuous mind ; urged by the love of God the Father in providing a Saviour, and giving him as a propitiatory sacrifice for sin ; by the dying love and compassion of God the Son ; and by the glories of heaven and the terrors of hell, to accept of that salvation which was procured, by a bleeding Saviour, on Calvary's mount. They are also urged to accept the terms of the gospel, and become reconciled to God, by the operation of the Holy Spirit on their hearts. All these, and many other things, are proposed to the consideration of sinners, in the preaching of the word : therefore, however short the term of time, in which you are taught the way of life, and urged to a compliance with gospel requirements, that time is of great importance.

3d._ It is important, because those who refuse to hear and obey are hardened in sin. Under the means of grace, it is impossible for sinners to remain stationary. Evil men and seducers, yea, all impenitent sinners, under whatever means they may live, wax worse and worse. So long as sinners continue to slight gospel calls ; set at nought God's counsel and disregard his reproofs, they rapidly increase in hardness. The more frequently they are called, the less attention they manifest. The oftener they are threatened, the less they regard the threatening. Every compassionate call of God that is disregarded, and every denunciation of wrath that is contemned, serves to increase the weight of guilt, and sink the sinner into hardness of heart, and blindness of mind. Stupidity and insensibility increase in some proportion to the number of calls disregarded, and commands disobeyed. After long continued courses of disobedience, conscience will become less faithful ; and the sinner will commit iniquity with less remorse. That every voluntary act of disobedience serves to harden the heart, and render the sinner's case more awfully hazardous, is evident from facts or examples, too frequently before our eyes, and also from scripture testimony. " Can the Ethiopean change his skin, or the leopard his spots; then may ye also do good, that are accustomed to do evil. A solemn consideration to those who are continually rejecting the messages of God, and refusing obedience to the precepts of the gospel, brought them by the faithful ministers of Christ. A consideration that ought to excite every one to immediate repentance, faith and new obedience, lest he should become more " hardened through the deceitfulness of sin."

4th. The time of a minister's continuance with a people is important, because the faithful among them are built up in holiness. By a pious ministry, the righteous are nourished up in the way of life. In the sanctuary they learn more and more of God's character; of the extent and spirituality of his holy law; of the plan of grace by Jesus Christ; of the rich and distinguishing grace of God towards some of the guilty race of men; and are led to humility under a sense of their unworthiness and ill-desert. They are also brought to adore and glorify that holy Being who hath, in sovereign love and compassion, delivered them out of the darkness and defilement of sin, placed them in the light of his countenance, and adorned them with the spotless robe of Christ's righteousness. With an abiding impression of these truths on their minds, they see the importance of a holy walk, and are animated to live as blamelessly as possible, in an observance of all the ordinances and statutes of the Lord. Their delight is in the law of the Lord; and the word of God is sweet to their souls. The meek will God teach his way; and his word will do good to the upright. " It pleaseth God by the foolishness of preaching to save them that believe." Through the instrumentality of the word preached, God is building up true believers in holiness, and preparing them to be pillars in the temple above: therefore, to them, every opportunity to hear the word of life is important and highly valuable.

5th. Another thing that makes the time of a

minister's continuance among a people important, however short it may be, is, the future happiness or misery of all who hear, is infinitely concerned.

The faithful minister of Christ will feel, in some good measure, the weight of his charge; and, knowing the consequences of his ministry will extend into eternity, he must be desirous of feeding his people with knowledge, and of instructing them into the most important doctrines in Christian theology. He will not attempt to amuse them with things of no profit, but will endeavor to teach them the way of life truly. The word preached will be, as an apostle expresseth it, " either a savor of life unto life, or of death unto death," to those who hear. Under the means with which God is pleased to favour people, they are forming characters for eternity; are training up, under the nurturing influences of divine ordinances, for that society which will eternally increase in holiness and happiness; or under all the means God is using with them, are ripening for a more awful and aggravated condemnation, at the last day; at which solemn period they will be sentenced to depart into everlasting fire, where shall be weeping and gnashing of teeth; and where the smoke of their torment will ascend forever and ever. How important, then, is even the shortest space of time people enjoy the ministry of reconciliation.

APPLICATION.

1. We are led to reflect, as well in view of our subject, as on this particular occasion, on the relation which hath subsisted between us. I have been among you, as your pastor and teacher, for the space of one year and six months. And with what fidelity I have fulfilled my duty to you, as a teacher of the way of life, God is witness, and ye are witnesses. But the connexion is now dissolved : therefore,

2. Serious examination becometh us. It becomes me to examine with seriousness, how I have discharged my duty as a watchman on this important part of the wall of God's spiritual Jerusalem; and

with what views. Although I may not have dwelt, distinctly, upon every particular doctrine and precept of God's word; yet I trust, you can bear me witness, that they have been brought to view, and their importance described. The character of the Triune God, as a holy sovereign, " having mercy on whom he will have mercy," and hardening whom he will; the character of man as an apostate from God, destitute of every degree of holiness, and possessing a " carnal mind, which is enmity against God;" the importance of regeneration, wrought by the special agency of the Holy Ghost; the necessity of immediate repentance and faith; and of a gospel walk, have been exhibited, as the subjects which have been under consideration, will testify. The feelings and the exercises of the real child of God have been very particularly and repeatedly described, as being in the preacher's apprehension, better calculated to force conviction upon the mind of a sinner, of his being totally destitute of a Christian temper, than any other one method that could be adopted. Although the increase is wholly of God, and ministers cannot cause one soul to repent and believe; yet, your preacher hath not considered that as any reason why he should relax his exertions; but rather as a stimulus to be faithful in duty, and to look to God, that he would appear for your help, that you perish not. He hath, it is believed, in some measure, felt the importance of obeying that command, " Go and preach unto them the preaching that I bid thee," and he hath been willing to leave the issue with him who is the sovereign Disposer of events. Yet he seeth great occasion, and desireth to be humble, that he hath been no more engaged and importunate in urging sinners to become reconciled to God. O God! pardon thy servant! Brethren, forgive him this wrong.

Serious examination also becometh *you*, once the people of my charge. Hath it been your hearty desire to gain instruction in the great things which

relate to the glory of God, and the everlasting felicity of your own souls; that you might better understand your duty, and bring a greater revenue of
glory to your Lord, by a stricter walk, and a more
uniform obedience to his precepts and commands?
—That you might obtain more light and knowledge, and be enabled the better to recommend the
religion professed and taught among you, to those
with whom you are connected; and that you might
cause an example of holy obedience to shine more
equally and increasingly bright before others, that
they, beholding you labour of love and good works,
might be induced to glorify your and their Father,
who is in heaven? Hath it been the rejoicing of
your hearts, at the return of every Lord's day, to
appear in the assembly of his people, and here unite
in the solemnities of divine worship? Hath it been
your grief, when you have been necessarily detained
from divine service?

Have you been made sensible of your lost and
criminal condition as sinners against God? Or are
you still regardless of the God who made you, and
lightly esteeming the Rock of your salvation? It
certainly becomes you to examine how the case now
stands between God and your souls. What improvement have you made of my ministrations, dur-
ing the period of a year and six months, in which
I have been "teaching the word of God among
you?" Have you been "nourished up in the words
of faith," and been made more spiritual, and more
heavenly minded? If so, you have reason to rejoice
and give glory to God; and to manifest by your
future life and conversation the high sense you en-
tertain of God's goodness, in giving you so long a
standing in his vineyard. But if you find, on examination, that you have not profited by the word
preached, and that you are still under the power of
an evil heart; strangers to experimental religion,
your case is truly alarming; and you ought to
make no delay, but haste for your lives to the city
of refuge, before the avenger of blood overtake you.

Linger not a moment longer in the meads of fasci-
nating pleasures, lest you be surfeited and sink down
into the lap of every sinful indulgence, and at last
awake from your reveries, in the fire that never shall
be quenched.

The consequences of the connexion which hath
subsisted between us are important; and they will
be eternal. They will be for the glory of God;
and if we have been actuated by pure motives, and
have faithfully performed the duties incumbent on
us respectively, our holiness and happiness will be
promoted in this world, and in the world to come,
our endless felicity. But if we have been governed,
in our conduct in this connexion, by selfish views,
and to promote unsuitable purposes, or to obtain any
sinister objects, the consequences will be no less important; for even in that case, God will be glorified,
and his justice wonderfully displayed, in our endless
destruction, unless we improve the present time in
deep humiliation and hearty repentance. It therefore becomes each of us, with much prayerfulness
and deep searchings of heart, to review every part
of our conduct; how, and with what views I have
taught the word of God among you; and how you
have heard and profited by it. Let us ask forgive-
ness of God, in every thing in which we have
come short of our duty; and heartily seek his direction and assistance in all our future conduct.

3. Our subject affords consolation under many of
the changes through which we are called to pass on
our journey through this world. It supposeth there
may be changes, and frequent changes of ministers.
Paul, though caressed and beloved by all the friends of
Jesus where he was called to preach the gospel of the
· kingdom, was not allowed to continue long in any one
place, God having important purposes to answer by
his removal. Thus it hath been in every succeeding
period of the church. If ministers of Christ have not
generally been removed from place to place, as were
the apostles in the first ages of the Christian era; yet
changes have frequently taken place. Owing to va-

rious causes, ministers have been separated from their people, suddenly ; and hot unfrequently by death. But under such adverse scenes of Providence, if people place their happiness in the highest good of God's kingdom, it will be the ultimate object of every right desire of their hearts. However dark the dispensations of heaven may be, yet the pious mind will remain in peace ; knowing all events are ordered by the Lord ; and will, in the general issue, terminate for the good of the universe. It will rejoice, because " the Lord God omnipotent reigneth."

It is of small consequence, my brethren, by whom, if the *word of God* be really *taught* and *obeyed.* Paul may plant, and Apollos may water, in vain, unless God should give the increase. Christians are God's workmanship ; and it is of no great consequence, by what instruments he carries on his work. If the pure doctrines of the gospel are taught and obeyed, God will be glorified, and souls trained up, by divine influences, into a meetness for heavenly joys. Although it is of little consequence by whom the word is faithfully taught, yet you may expect that minister will be unfaithful, who has not an experimental acquaintance with divine things : therefore, it is important that every minister should have the love of God a ruling principle in his heart ; as this would lead him to fidelity in the discharge of ministerial duties.

I hope you may, through the blessing of God on your endeavours, obtain a pastor, who will be made an instrument of greater good in the cause of Christ and of souls, than I have been ; one who may be made by the great Head of the church, a burning and shining light in this golden candlestick ; and may many here rejoice in his light. May you have the consolation of receiving one who shall more than restore the breach that is now made ; one who will manifest, by his preaching and conversation, that the love of God is a ruling principle in his heart, and that his greatest desire is to promote the glory of his Lord and Master, in the salvation of your souls.

4. As my relation to you is now dissolved, by a venerable ecclesiastical council, mutually chosen ; let me exhort you, in view of this subject, to make all laudable exertions to obtain a minister who will preach the word of God in the manner that hath been mentioned.

The settlement of a gospel minister is one of the most important transactions in which a people can be employed in this life. It is important to the minister himself, and important to the people with whom he is connected, because eternal consequences are depending. In settling a minister, let me beseech you, to have a particular regard to experimental piety, exemplary conduct, and sound doctrine. Although you cannot certainly know the heart, yet you may learn something respecting its exercises, by the external conduct and conversation, and the doctrines a minister may inculcate. Beware of one who does not bring into view the great and leading doctrines of the gospel; one who saith little or nothing respecting the pure and holy character of God, the divinity of Christ, and the atonement he hath made ; one who is silent on the doctrines of sovereign grace, on man's natural enmity against God, and the necessity of a change of heart, wrought, not by light or moral suasion, but by the special agency of the Holy Spirit : for you may rest assured, that he, who doth not openly avow these sentiments, but keepeth them out of sight, in his preaching and conversation, neglecteth those parts of his duty which are most important, and giveth just occasion for you to suspect he has not an experimental acquaintance with the awful depravity of the human heart, and that he is a stranger to the work of grace on his own soul ; and indeed, that he hath very imperfect, if any, ideas of the infinite importance of vital piety.

Take heed that ye be not deceived in this highly interesting business of choosing a minister. You must not be governed, in this matter, by a desire to obtain one who will help to amuse you in the ways

and practices of sin, and to keep conscience from being awaked to an execution of her office; one who
will prophesy smooth things, and make the way to
heaven so easy, that it will be almost if not quite
impossible to fall short of eternal bliss : for, the touch
of such an one is poison, and his embrace is death.

Let it be your earnest solicitude to obtain a spiritual guide and instructor, who will with prudence
and plainness show you the right way of the Lord :
who will point out your sin and danger, and lead you
to the ever full and ever flowing fountain of Christ's
blood for pardon and for cleansing ; one who will
not shun to declare unto you the whole revealed
counsel of God ; who will faithfully warn you not
to trust in your own doings for salvation, but in the
mercy of God, through the merits of Jesus Christ :
one who will not only be apostolic in his preaching,
but holy and heavenly in his life and conversation :
one who will cordially comply with the apostolic
exhortation, and show himself " a pattern of good
works ; in doctrine showing uncorruptness, gravity,
sincerity,—sound speech that cannot be condemned ; that he who is of the contrary part may be
ashamed, having no evil thing to say of him."

Having, by the blessing of God on your endeavours, obtained such an one to minister to you in
holy things, pay constant attendance upon, and attention to, his instructions. "Forsake not the assem-
bling of yourselves together, as the manner of some
is :" for, should you forsake the house of worship,
you will discourage your minister, and give him
melancholy occasion to complain, in the language of
the prophet, " I have laboured in vain, I have spent
my strength for nought, and in vain." Let him
see, and have evidence, by your constant and serious
attendance upon his teaching, and by your holy conversation and exemplary walk, that you profit by
his labours ; and that you " esteem him very highly
in love for his works' sake." Let not his instructions fall upon you, like seed by the way-side, or
upon a rock ; but may they find an entrance into

good and honest hearts, that fruit, in rich abundance, may be produced to the glory of God, the divine Husbandman, and to your unspeakable peace and endless happiness. Your dearest, your immortal interests are concerned, in a right improvement of all ministerial instructions. Be wise in time for eternity.

Your aged and venerable pastor, who has grown grey in your service, although unable to instruct you from this sacred desk, yet can do it in private conversation ; and he must certainly feel himself bound, by the most sacred ties, to watch for souls as one who must give account : and you are under no less solemn obligations to hear, receive and obey his scriptural instructions. Be not forgetful of those truths you have repeatedly heard from his lips ; but may he observe them having influence on your hearts and lives. May he continue to experience your kindnesses which have been numerous ; his declining sun set in smiles ; and his falling mantle rest on some Elisha who shall be bold in the Lord to declare unto you the messages of heaven ; whose example shall be luminous, and whose conversation such as becometh the gospel of God our Saviour.

Let no root of bitterness be suffered to spring up to trouble you. " Be at peace among yourselves." " Be perfect, be of good comfort, be of one mind, live in peace ; and the God of love and peace shall be with you."

Whilst I bid adieu to the dear children of God who are training up, through the nurturing influences of divine ordinances, for heavenly glory, I do it with feelings very different from those I experience when taking leave of those of you who are yet in your sins ; strangers to the pure pleasures of religion, and exposed every moment to all the awful horrors of endless destruction. O precious immortals ! suffer me, for the last time, and as it were with my expiring breath, to beseech every impenitent sinner present, whether *old* or *young*, *parent* or *child*, *professor* or *non-professor*, " in Christ's stead," to become, immediately, " reconciled to God."

After departing from this house of worship, at this time, your next meeting may be at the solemn bar of your omniscient Judge. Do you ever reflect, with due seriousness, that the last great day is near; when that divine Jesus, whom you now reject with scorn and derision, will come to judgment? Hark! do you not hear his chariot-wheels? Cast your eyes upward! see the heavens opened! behold the God Christ Jesus, seated on a cloud, moving with majesty towards this earth; attended with myriads of angelic hosts. Hark! the trumpet sounds, in language articulate, Arise ye dead, and come ye living, to meet your Judge! My fellow sinners and fellow immortals, are you ready to hear and attend to the solemn call? If you be, you will ascend to meet the Lord in the air, and thus be ever with the Lord. But if not prepared, by grace, for that important summons, your sentence will be, " Depart, ye cursed, into everlasting fire, prepared for the devil and his angels." Is this a final sentence? Yes: it will never be reversed. Can you endure it? Dare you make the trial? or do you feel somewhat concerned to make your escape from this awful doom? Let me inform you, then, for the last time, that there is no way of escape, but by fleeing to the purifying blood of Christ, experiencing a change of heart, and being united in love to the Lord Jesus; clothed with his righteousness, received by faith. That you may, now while you are prisoners of hope, attend to divine calls, turn to the strong hold of the gospel, and find sanctuary in Christ; and that you may all be prepared to meet in the unchanging temple above, 'to unite with all the redeemed from among men, in ascriptions of thanksgiving to him who hath washed you in his own blood, is the earnest prayer of your servant, for Christ's sake, who now bids you a most affectionate *Farewell.* Amen and Amen.